HELEN KELLER

Troll Associates

HELEN KELLER

by Laurence Santrey

Illustrated by Hal Frenck

Troll Associates

Library of Congress Cataloging in Publication Data

Santrey, Laurence.
  Helen Keller.

  Summary: A biography of the blind and deaf woman
who overcame her handicaps with the help of her
teacher, Anne Sullivan.
    1. Keller, Helen, 1880-1968—Juvenile literature.
2. Blind-deaf—United States—Biography—Juvenile
literature.   3. Blind-deaf—Education—United States—
Juvenile literature.   4. Sullivan, Annie, 1866-1936—
Juvenile literature.   [1. Keller, Helen, 1880-1968.
2. Blind-deaf.   3. Deaf.   4. Physically handicapped]
I. Frenck, Hal, ill.   II. Title.
HV1624.K4S26   1984   362.410924 [B]   84-2682
ISBN 0-8167-0156-3 (lib. bdg.)
ISBN 0-8167-0157-1 (pbk.)

Blind and deaf, Helen Keller lived in a world of darkness and silence. But these terrible handicaps could not crush her spirit. Her warmth as a human being, her intelligence, and her magnificent accomplishments were an inspiration to those who knew her. And her story continues to inspire all those who hear it.

When Helen Keller was born on June 27, 1880, her hearing and eyesight were normal. She heard the birds sing on the farm where she lived in Tuscumbia, Alabama. She saw the smiles of her parents and the broad, green fields around her home. Helen was a cheerful baby, and it was obvious right away that she was very intelligent.

Then, when Helen was one-and-a-half years old, she came down with a serious illness. It isn't known what the illness was, only that it gave Helen a high fever that lasted for a few days. She was so sick that her parents were afraid that she might not live. Then, at last, the fever broke and the little girl recovered. But the illness left her blind and deaf.

Mr. and Mrs. Keller hoped that these handicaps would pass in time. Sometimes they would test Helen's hearing and vision, by clapping their hands sharply or holding up a lighted lamp. But the little golden-haired child did not respond to the sound or the light. The Kellers finally had to accept the truth—Helen would never see or hear again.

Helen's parents knew that their little girl

was smart, yet they had no way of teaching her or even communicating with her. They did the best they could, giving her love, attention, and the freedom to do anything she wanted. Even so, there was not much happiness in Helen's life. As she later explained, it was like being locked up alone in a silent, black room, with no way out and no way to express her feelings.

When Helen was five years old, Mrs. Keller read about a woman named Laura Bridgman. Miss Bridgman also was blind and deaf. Yet she had been taught to read, write, and communicate with others by using a finger alphabet. She had learned these skills at the Perkins Institute for the Blind in Boston, Massachusetts. Laura Bridgman's story gave new hope to the Kellers. Perhaps there was a way to help Helen, after all.

The Kellers took Helen to see Dr. Alexander Graham Bell. While Dr. Bell is best known for inventing the telephone, he also founded a school to train teachers for the deaf. Dr. Bell suggested that the Kellers write to the Perkins Institute, asking for a teacher to work with their daughter. They followed Dr. Bell's advice. Not long after, on March 3, 1887, Helen's teacher arrived at the Keller house. Her name was Anne Sullivan.

Although Helen was excited by having a newcomer in the house, she was also confused. Her new teacher—unlike her parents—did not let Helen do whatever she wanted to do whenever she wanted to do it. Helen was not allowed to put her fingers into everyone's food or have temper tantrums when she didn't get her way. Anne Sullivan knew that Helen's behavior was wild simply because she hadn't been taught to act properly. Therefore, Anne's first job as Helen's teacher would be to teach the girl to act like a civilized human being.

Anne Sullivan wanted to teach Helen to wash her hands and to comb her hair. She also wanted the child to learn not to scream and kick when she was denied something. But the Kellers did not follow the teacher's rules. They could not bring themselves to discipline their daughter.

Finally, Anne Sullivan proposed a solution. There was a small house on the grounds of the Keller farm. She wanted to move into it with Helen and work with her there—alone. The Kellers reluctantly agreed.

The first few days in the little house were horrible for both teacher and student. Helen could not understand why she had been taken away from her parents and home. But in a week, she began to respond to her teacher. And within two weeks, they were friends. Once this was accomplished, the little girl began to learn words.

Helen's first word was "doll." Anne began by putting a doll in Helen's arms. Then she took Helen's right hand and tapped out the letters *d-o-l-l* in the finger alphabet. She tapped out the word again and again.

Later that day, she gave Helen a piece of cake and spelled the word "cake" in Helen's hand. Then the little girl took her teacher's hand and spelled *c-a-k-e!* Anne was overjoyed and gave her young student a piece of cake as a reward. The first step had been taken in the child's education.

But Helen didn't understand that the finger-tapping was actually spelling words. The little girl was only imitating a series of finger motions. It was like a parrot repeating words without having any idea of what it is saying. But Anne kept on working with Helen until, on the morning of April 5, 1887, a great breakthrough took place.

Anne Sullivan described it this way: "We went out to the pump house, and I made Helen hold her hands under the spout while I pumped. I spelled *w-a-t-e-r* into her free hand.... The word coming so close upon the sensation of cold water rushing over her hand seemed to startle her. She dropped the mug and stood transfixed. A new light came into her face. She spelled *w-a-t-e-r* several times."

After that, Helen reached down and touched the ground. Anne spelled *g-r-o-u-n-d* in Helen's hand. Helen pointed to Anne, and Anne spelled *t-e-a-c-h-e-r*. From that day on, "Teacher" was Helen's name for Anne.

Helen spent the rest of that fantastic day learning words. She learned the words "mother" and "baby." She also learned the names of many objects in the house, the name of the family dog, and her own name. Mr. and Mrs. Keller were delighted. But their delight was mild compared to the thrill felt by teacher and student!

Seven-year-old Helen spent every waking moment learning about the world. Anne could hardly keep up with Helen's demands for more and more information. To help Helen learn faster, Anne taught her to read and write in braille. Braille is a way of printing words by using raised dots on paper. The method was invented by Louis Braille, in 1829, to enable blind people to read by touch. Helen quickly mastered braille and began a lifetime of avid reading and writing.

In the spring of 1888, when Helen was eight years old, she and Anne Sullivan went to Boston. There, at the Perkins Institute, Helen studied Latin, German, Greek, French, English, arithmetic, geography, and zoology. Anne sat beside her in every class, spelling out the instructor's words in Helen's hand. Together, Helen and Anne spent ten school years at Perkins.

In those years, Helen also learned to
speak words out loud. It was a difficult
thing to do. Helen began by placing her
hand on her instructor's mouth, to feel the
way words are formed. Then, Helen tried to
copy these actions. Because she could not
hear her own voice, the young girl could
not know if she was doing it right. But Anne
worked with her day and night, until Helen
could speak clearly.

Helen soon acquired a new goal. She wanted to go to college. And so, in order to take the long examinations this would require, Helen learned to type. With this new skill, she passed a nine-hour test and was accepted into Radcliffe College. There, with Anne always at her side, Helen did extremely well. She graduated from Radcliffe with honors in English and German and credit in advanced Latin.

Even before Helen Keller finished college, she became well known for her extraordinary achievements. Her example inspired others who were handicapped to keep trying, no matter how hard it might be. Her example also inspired people to support education for the handicapped. Indeed, this became Helen's work for the rest of her life —to tell her story and to help others.

In the years that followed, Helen traveled around the world, speaking to people in many countries. She also wrote a number of books and magazine articles about her childhood, her education, and her devoted teacher, Anne Sullivan, who was with her every step of the way. Anne was Helen's eyes and ears, as well as her closest friend.

When Anne Sullivan died, in 1936, a woman named Polly Thompson took her place at Helen's side. Polly and Helen continued Helen's life work. During World War II, Helen and Polly visited American troops who had been wounded in battle. Helen gave them courage by being her warm, cheerful, friendly self. Meeting her filled many of these soldiers with faith in their own futures.

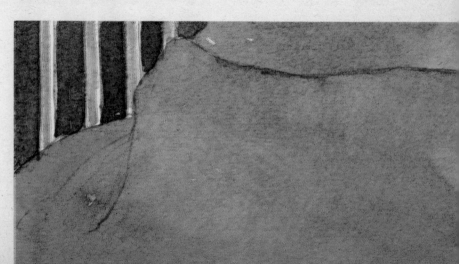

After the war, through the Helen Keller World Crusade, she worked to help blind and deaf children everywhere. Though she was growing frail, Helen traveled all over, making speeches and raising funds for the benefit of others. Then, in 1961, Helen suf-

fered a mild stroke, which left her very weak.

Helen Keller was no longer able to fly from country to country, making appearances. But she went on writing, giving interviews, and raising money for the American Foundation for the Blind.

When Helen Keller died—on June 1, 1968 —the world lost a great treasure. This unique woman, who lived in perpetual darkness and silence, had brought beauty and light to countless human beings. And her story has continued to inspire many more in the years since then.